Shelter Pet

By Peggy DeLapp

An animal shelter is a good place to look for a new pet. Read this book to learn how an animal shelter can help you find a pet.

PEARSON

🟧 Is your family planning to get a pet? Maybe you can find one at an animal **shelter**. Many towns and cities have animal shelters.

- People take care of pets at an animal **shelter**.

> 🟧 A vet helps the animals stay healthy.

🔶 Why are animals in a shelter? Sometimes people can't keep their pets. They might move to a place where they can't have animals. They can bring their pets to a shelter.

🔶 This person gives her pet to someone who works at a shelter.

- Sometimes pets get lost. People from shelters help lost pets.

- This person is helping a lost pet.

🔶 There are millions of dogs and cats in shelters. These dogs and cats need a home. They need someone to **adopt** them.

🔶 **Kitten Season**

Most kittens are born in spring and summer. Summer is a good time to adopt a cat or kitten.

● Your family may want to **adopt** a pet. You can give the pet a new home.

● You can learn how to take care of your new pet.

🔶 Animal shelters have different kinds of animals. Most shelters have dogs, cats, puppies, and kittens.

● You may see some small pets at a shelter. They need homes, too.

🔶 You will see people working at the shelter. Some of them are **volunteers**. These volunteers love taking care of animals.

🟢 Some volunteers walk the dogs and play with them.

- The **volunteers** can help you find a pet. You can see the pets. You can get to know them.

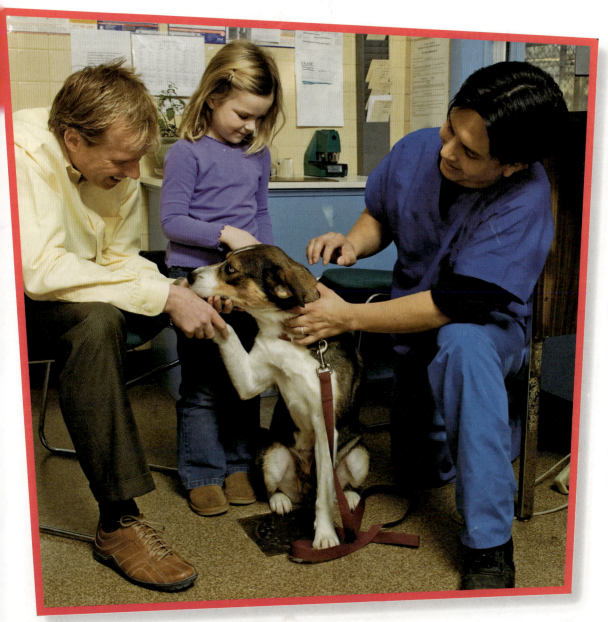

🔶 Shelters have **adult** and baby animals. Baby animals may need more care than adult animals. Baby animals need to learn how to live with people.

🟢 It can be hard to train a puppy!

● **Adult** animals can be great pets. They can make people happy.

Most older dogs are calmer than puppies.

🔶 At a shelter, you and your family can find a pet that is just right for you. The people at the shelter will help you. They will tell you how to take care of your new pet.

● Your pet will be happy to have a home. It will love its new family. You will love your new pet, too.

Glossary

adopt to take into the family

adult a grown-up

shelter a place that takes care of animals that need homes

volunteers people who work but do not get paid